Sustainable Planet

ANNA CLAYBOURNE

FRANKLIN WATTS
LONDON • SYDNEY

Franklin Watts
First published in Great Britain in 2022 by the Watts Publishing Group
Copyright © the Watts Publishing Group 2022

Editors: Annabel Savery & Julia Bird
Designer: Rocket Design (East Anglia) Ltd

Alamy: Dinodia 19t; Motoring Picture Library 8bl; Science History Images 7tr;
World History Archive 10bl.
Getty Images: Alfred Eisenstaedt/LIFE 11c; Jill Ferry Photography 32t; Pauline Lewis 31b.
Shutterstock: Lillia_A 27tl; Acrylik Vectors 16tl; Alfmaler 6c, 33t, 33br; Alewiena design 10-11bg; Sira Anamwong 9t; Antishock 29br; Tatiana Arestova 7bl; Artitok 23tr; asm.prod 17tr; Nadezda Barkova 27tr, 31tr; Benchart 30-31b; Andrii Bezvershenko 32bc, 33crb; Iryna Bidovska 30c; Bilbadash 41cl; Ilya Bolotov 17tcb; Boyko Pictures 42tl; BRO vector 17b, 40bl; Catandchild 41t; ChameleonsEye 11bc; Ivan Chudakov 41br; Colorlife 27cr; Curiosity 10-11bg; Cute.flat 18t; Doremi 5tl; Oleksandr Derevianko 25c; Dukesn 16bl; Egirin 12br; Evellean 13cl; Everett Collection 6bl, 6br; Faber14 13bl; Faberr Ink 23tl; Ryan Fletcher 26c; Flower travelin man 14bl, 14bc, 15t, 15cl; Frantic00 7tl; Dacian G 17tc; Gaidamashchuk 18c; Good Stock 1c, 3t,13tl, 13bc,14br, 15c, 15cr, 34cl, 34b,38-39b, 39cr, 40br, 43tr; GraficsRF.com 32b, 33cl, 33cr;Ken Griffiths 29r; Francisco Sandoval Guate 30t;Gvardgraph 28cr; Happy Pictures 5cl; Helgascandinavus 41cr; Helterskelter 43cr ;Ian Hitchcock 15b; Mikhail Hoika 18cr; Iconic Bestiary 8t, 12t, 13cr, 18cl;i Draw 4crb; Anna Illustrator 12cr; innnot 20b; Inspiring 37t; Sarawut Itsaranuwut 10t;Ivector 13c; 39tl, 42c; Hayoung Jeon/EPA-EFE/Rex 37b; G Jordison 31tl; Ilya Kalinin 19br; Iurii Killian 16cr; Angelina Ko 16cl; Darya Kozlova 43br; Viktoria Kurpas 42b; Janos Levente 4tr, 5bl; Linefab Portfolio 4-5c; LivDeco 1bg; Logiart 28ca; Magnia 24-25b; Don Mammoser 29b; Man C 39tc; Marish 47; Maxart 17tl; Merggy 21t; Mhatzapa 17tcl;MicroOne 2-3b, 4cr, 4br, 6tl, 26-27b; Mix3r 35t; MuchMania 8-9b;Naum 5c;Netkoff 16c; Kate Nikelser 34-35 border; NTL Studio 34cr;Oceloti 22b;Yulia Ogneva 34t; Olha1981 22t; Onimate 12cl; Maciej Olszewski 24c;PCH Vector 14c; Petia_is 24t; Petovarga 16br, 26t, 35b; Pizzastereo 19tr;ProStockStudio 39tr, 39cl; Eduard Radu 6cr; RaiDztor 20t; Ridhobadal 7bc;Teerapat Santitad 28br; Save Jungle 28cl; Scharfsinn 31c; Seahorse Vector 23bl, 23br, 42-43c;Elena Sharipova 36r; SkyPics Studio 4trb; Richard G Smith 11t; Irina Streinikova 17c; Olga Streinkova 12bl; Sunnydream 33c;Tristan Tan 28c;Tarikdiz 30cl;TeraVector 9b;Tgart2nd 10c;Toltemara 19cr; Tomacco 28bc; Triff 11br; Vector illustration 6-7bg; Vectorlab20 9c; Vector Mine 25t,36b; Vectorpic 27cl; Vector Show 29bc; Venimo 13tr; White space illustrations 30cr; Shamar Whyte 5br; Peter J Wilson 21b; Yusufdemirci 2c, 14t; YummyBuum 18br; Zunaki 20bg; Zzveillust 14cbg.
Wellcome Collection/CCA.CC BY 4.0 19tc.

Every effort has been made to clear copyright. Should there be any inadvertent omission,
please apply to the publisher for rectification.

HB ISBN: 978 1 4451 7757 1

PB ISBN: 978 1 4451 7758 8

Printed in Dubai

MIX
Paper from
responsible sources
FSC® C104740
FSC
www.fsc.org

Franklin Watts
An imprint of
Hachette Children's Group
Part of the Watts Publishing Group
Carmelite House
50 Victoria Embankment
London EC4Y 0DZ

An Hachette UK Company
www.hachettechildrens.co.uk
www.franklinwatts.co.uk

All facts and statistics were correct
at the time of going to press.

CONTENTS

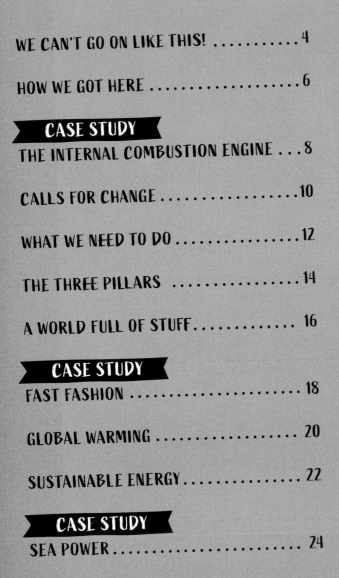

WE CAN'T GO ON LIKE THIS!

Since humans have existed on Earth, we've made BIG changes to our planet. We've built roads, towns and cities, and replaced forests with farms. We've littered the land with waste and polluted the sea and air. And we're still doing it.

★ We are using up natural resources, such as wood, minerals, oil and fish.

If we carry on using them up, they'll run out.

THE HUMAN PROBLEM

Of course, not everything humans do is bad. But a lot of the changes we've made do cause problems. If we don't change the way we live, we could be heading for disaster.

★ We are taking over wild land for farms, cities and roads.

If we take it all, there will be no wilderness left for wildlife, or for us either.

HELP

IT'S UNSUSTAINABLE!

Living like this is unsustainable – which simply means we can't sustain, or continue it.

Instead, we need to become sustainable! That means:

★ Using only what we can replace

★ Reusing and recycling waste, instead of dumping it

★ Reducing pollution – and cleaning up pollution that's already there

★ Living in a way in which we can carry on living, now and in the future.

★ We create waste that clutters up and pollutes the planet.

There's a limited amount of space to put waste in, and some waste is harmful.

MAKING THE CHANGES

To change, we have to do things differently. This includes the ways we work, travel, eat, spend money and use energy. It's a huge task, but we have already started to make changes, and everyone can help.

★ We burn fuel in cars, planes, factories and power stations, leading to global warming.

If we don't control global warming, climate change could make many parts of the Earth impossible to live in.

THIS BOOK IS ALL ABOUT HOW ...

HOW WE GOT HERE

The world wasn't always like this. Long ago, there were far fewer humans and we didn't cause so many problems for the planet. So, what happened? Follow the timeline to find out.

AT LEAST 3.8 BILLION YEARS AGO

First life on Earth

800 MILLION YEARS AGO

First animals

Dinosaurs

241–66 MILLION YEARS AGO

The first early humans

2 MILLION YEARS AGO

Paper

2,000 YEARS AGO

The wheel

5,500 YEARS AGO

Steam engine

THE INDUSTRIAL REVOLUTION

Around 250 years ago, the Industrial Revolution saw an especially important change. We began making most things in factories, and many people moved to big cities.

250 YEARS AGO

HUMAN POPULATION: ABOUT 1 BILLION

Planes

Electric battery

220 YEARS AGO

120 YEARS AGO

Modern humans (Homo sapiens, the same species as us)

EARLY HUMANS

Early humans lived in small groups, hunted wild animals and gathered food from the land. Over time, we learnt to make tools, pottery, clothes and huts, and discovered cooking methods.

The first farmers

300,000 YEARS AGO

12,000 YEARS AGO

> Humans have existed for only two million years – a tiny fraction of the history of life on Earth.

FARMING BEGAN

Eventually, people started settling in one place, growing plants and keeping animals for food. Humans began living in bigger groups, creating villages, towns and cities.

CHANGES OF THE HOLOCENE

The last 12,000 years or so are known as the Holocene epoch (or time period). During this time, our amazing ability to imagine, create and build has led to all kinds of inventions: vehicles, engines, factories, electric gadgets, modern medicine and computers.

HUMAN POPULATION: ABOUT 4 MILLION

PEOPLE EVERYWHERE!

Thanks to all these changes, life became easier, more people were born and lived longer, and the human population grew. We needed more towns, cities, farms, cars and electricity. We took up more space and created more and more pollution – and that's how we got here!

TODAY!

90 YEARS AGO

30 YEARS AGO

Antibiotics

Global internet

HUMAN POPULATION: ABOUT 7.8 BILLION

7

THE INTERNAL COMBUSTION ENGINE

The internal combustion engine is a great example of a clever invention that changed the world - but also ended up causing serious problems.

Internal combustion engine

WHAT IS IT?

You might not have heard of the internal combustion engine, but you've almost certainly travelled in a vehicle powered by one! It's the type of engine that makes most cars work. They're also found in motorbikes, vans, trucks and some planes and boats.

In 1885, German inventor Carl Benz used his own internal combustion engine design in his new 'Benz Motorwagen', an early car.

Engine

ENGINE INVENTIONS

The first engines were steam engines, used to power factory machines and trains. Then, through the 18th and 19th centuries, several inventors experimented with internal combustion engines. These new, smaller engines burned (or combusted) fuel inside a container to make a pushing force. They could be used to power small, automatic vehicles – the first cars.

CAR CULTURE

When the first cars went on sale, only the rich could afford them. But before long, more businesses joined the car industry and began mass-producing affordable cars in factories. As more and more people bought cars, the world changed ...

CARS EVERYWHERE

There are now:

★ About 1.5 billion cars in the world, and over 2 billion internal combustion engines.

★ Over 65 million km of roads crisscrossing the Earth – enough to reach to the Moon and back 80 times.

★ CARS LET PEOPLE TRAVEL FAST AND EASILY SO THEY COULD DRIVE TO WORK OR THE SHOPS.

★ WE BEGAN DESIGNING CITIES, TOWNS AND HOMES AROUND CAR OWNERS.

★ MORE AND MORE GREEN SPACE WAS TURNED INTO ROADS AND CAR PARKS.

★ CARS BURNED FUEL MADE FROM OIL, PUMPING POLLUTION INTO THE AIR.

★ CAR ACCIDENTS HARMED MILLIONS OF PEOPLE – AND EVEN MORE ANIMALS.

TIME TO DO SOMETHING!

Cars are incredibly useful, but we now know that cars which burn fuel are not sustainable. We need to use better, less harmful ways to get around.

CALLS FOR CHANGE

Henry Thoreau

Today, most people know that the planet is in danger and that we have to act. That's thanks to all the campaigners, writers, scientists and politicians who have called for change.

EARLY WORRIES

Soon after the Industrial Revolution began in the 18th century, some people realised that all the new factories, engines and smoky cities could lead to problems. Writers such as American naturalist Henry Thoreau wrote about nature and the importance of the wilderness.

In wildness is the preservation of the world.

We must not waste what we have.

In 1896, Sweish scientist Svante Arrhenius calculated how burning more fuel could warm the Earth's climate. He wrote that humans would need 'new sources of energy that shall never become exhausted' – sustainable ones, in other words!

Svante Arrhenius

PROTECTING NATURE

In the 19th and 20th centuries, people started setting up nature reserves to keep habitats safe for wildlife, and environmentalists campaigned to protect endangered species.

Bird expert Rosalie Edge set up a wildlife reserve for birds of prey.

RISE OF THE GREEN MOVEMENT

After the Second World War ended in 1945, cities were rebuilt, populations grew and many people became wealthier. Car and plane travel, plastics and electrical gadgets became popular. As people began to realise how harmful this was for the planet, the green movement took off.

Green charities and organisations were launched, as well as Green political parties. Governments and international organisations, such as the United Nations, started taking action by making anti-pollution laws and sustainable development agreements.

In 1962, US biologist Rachel Carson's book *Silent Spring* described how human activities were harming nature – in particular the use of chemical pesticides on farms.

The environmental group Greenpeace used this ship, the *Rainbow Warrior*, to carry out protests and blockades against pollution and hunting.

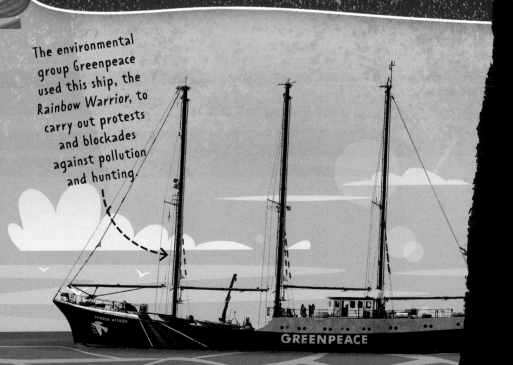

GREENPEACE

THE VIEW FROM SPACE

In the 1960s, astronauts went to space for the first time. We could now see Earth from space, and how small and delicate it looked. This inspired more people to want to protect it.

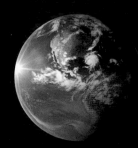

WHAT WE NEED TO DO

We have already started trying to undo the damage done to the planet, and switching to sustainable ways of living. But we're not there yet. We need to go a lot further, and faster, to make it happen.

CHANGING EVERYTHING

Becoming truly sustainable means changing many different aspects of life, work and behaviour. They are all interconnected and affect each other. Globally, we must all think about the following:

CONSUMERISM

Buying less stuff. Making things last longer and reusing, reselling or passing on old items

FACTORIES AND INDUSTRY

Using recycled materials instead of new raw materials and making better quality, longer-lasting items

WILD HABITATS

Returning more land to a wild state

JOBS

Creating more jobs in recycling, renewable energy and green transport. Working from home more to reduce travel

GREENHOUSE GASES AND GLOBAL WARMING

Reducing the production and release of greenhouse gases, and planting more trees and plants to absorb carbon dioxide from the air

RECYCLING

Recycling whatever we can, and making as many things recyclable as possible

POPULATION

Slowing down population growth and reducing human population long-term

POLLUTION

Reducing pollution of the planet. Cleaning up existing pollution and stopping the use of harmful plastics and chemicals

ENERGY

Reducing our energy needs and using only renewable energy sources

TRANSPORT

Travelling less, stopping burning fossil fuels and using low-pollution forms of transport

HOUSING

Designing homes to use less energy

FOOD AND FARMING

Switching from meat to crop farming, stopping transporting food long distances and combining farms with natural habitats

ALL ABOARD!

To do this, everyone has to be involved: from individuals to worldwide organisations. For example, think about reducing greenhouse gases:

★ Individuals make decisions, such as walking to work.

★ Scientists come up with solutions, such as artificial trees that soak up greenhouse gases.

★ Businesses choose green options, for example using electric delivery vehicles.

★ Governments and councils make towns and cities greener, for example by providing electric public transport and safe cycle paths.

★ Country leaders make laws, such as banning new diesel cars.

★ International organisations get countries to work together to agree on laws and targets for reducing greenhouse gases.

THE THREE PILLARS

You can think of sustainability as being made up of three main areas. They're often called the 'three pillars' of sustainability. They are:

SUSTAINABILITY

ECONOMIC

FACTORIES

BANKING

JOBS

BUYING AND SELLING

WEALTH AND POVERTY

ENVIRONMENTAL

HABITATS

WILDLIFE

SOIL

AIR

WATER

CLIMATE

SOCIAL

EQUALITY

JUSTICE

HEALTH

EDUCATION

HAPPINESS

STANDING TOGETHER

The 'three pillars' are all interlinked and work together. If we want to make something sustainable, it has to involve all three areas, or pillars, in order to work well.

ON YOUR BIKE!

As an example, think about one change that could make the world more sustainable – people switching to cycling instead of driving cars. You can see how it involves all the pillars, and each pillar affects the others.

ECONOMIC

★ More bike factories, fewer car factories

★ More jobs making, recycling, selling and fixing bikes

★ Countries and cities need more cycle paths and cycle parking

ENVIRONMENTAL

★ Cycle paths are safer for wildlife

★ Reduced greenhouse gases

★ Reduced pollution = better air quality

SOCIAL

★ Cleaner air means less asthma and other breathing problems

★ Exercise makes people healthier

★ Bikes are cheaper than cars, so people have more money for other things

FACT FILE

MORE BIKES

There are more cars than bikes in the world today, but eventually, that could change.

Number of bikes on the planet:
AROUND 1 BILLION

Country with the most bikes:
CHINA, WITH ABOUT 450 MILLION

Date the first pedal bicycle was invented: **1839**

A WORLD FULL OF STUFF

In the modern world, we're surrounded by STUFF. Whatever you want, if you have enough money, you can probably buy it in a shop or online.

STATIONERY

STUFF!

MAKE-UP

SPORTS GEAR

WHAT'S WRONG WITH STUFF?

Stuff isn't always bad. It's often useful and important. We need clothes, furniture and everyday items. Modern inventions such as smartphones and washing machines make life easier. It's part of our culture to enjoy things like fashion, music, sports and books.

The problem starts when there's too much stuff, as it causes problems for the planet.

Making new things uses up natural resources and energy.

Transporting goods around the world also uses energy, which adds to global warming.

Throwing stuff away creates waste that mostly ends up as litter, in landfill or being burned.

FASHION

GAMES
CONSOLES

PHONES

JEWELLERY

ELECTRICAL
GOODS

WHY DO WE DO IT?

That's a very good question!
It's human nature to like new,
interesting and cool things. But
another reason is because of
the world's economy – the way
businesses, jobs and money work.

Making, transporting and selling
stuff gives people jobs and makes
money for businesses. Consumers
(people who buy stuff) buy more than they need to
– often because social media, magazines, TV shows
and advertising makes people feel like they have to
have it!

The whole system works by making us
want more stuff all the time.

But we could do it differently by ...

★ Redesigning things so they last longer
and can be mended and reused.

★ Recycling everything, so that old
stuff is made into new stuff.

★ Learning to live with less stuff,
and looking after it better.

FACT FILE

WHAT MAKES
US HAPPY?

Scientists have found that new stuff
doesn't make us as happy as we think
it will! In fact, in studies, these things
were the best at making people happy:

★ Family and friends

★ Having a job you like

★ Helping other people.

FAST FASHION

Today, most people, at least in the world's wealthier countries, have far more clothes than they need. They can afford them because clothes are much cheaper than they once were.

We started wearing animal-skin clothes more than 100,000 years ago!

Early fabrics were made from woven wool or linen.

100,000 YEARS AGO

10,000 YEARS AGO

2,500 YEARS AGO

The ancient Greeks wore linen tunics.

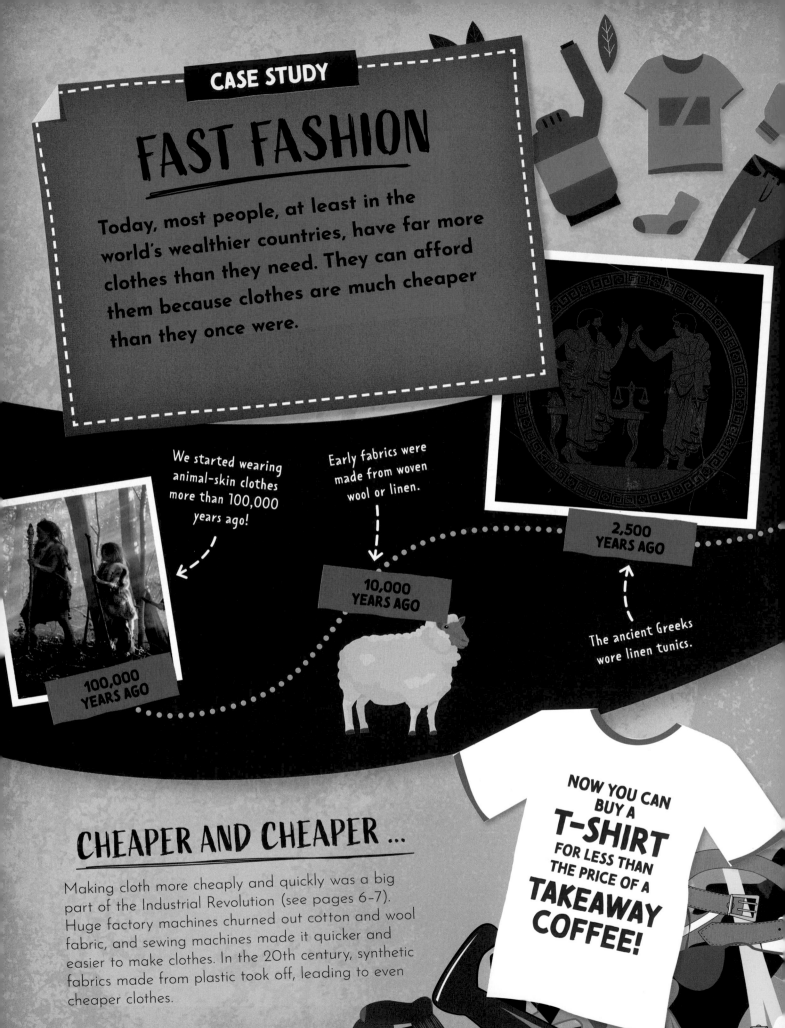

CHEAPER AND CHEAPER ...

Making cloth more cheaply and quickly was a big part of the Industrial Revolution (see pages 6–7). Huge factory machines churned out cotton and wool fabric, and sewing machines made it quicker and easier to make clothes. In the 20th century, synthetic fabrics made from plastic took off, leading to even cheaper clothes.

NOW YOU CAN BUY A **T-SHIRT** FOR LESS THAN THE PRICE OF A **TAKEAWAY COFFEE!**

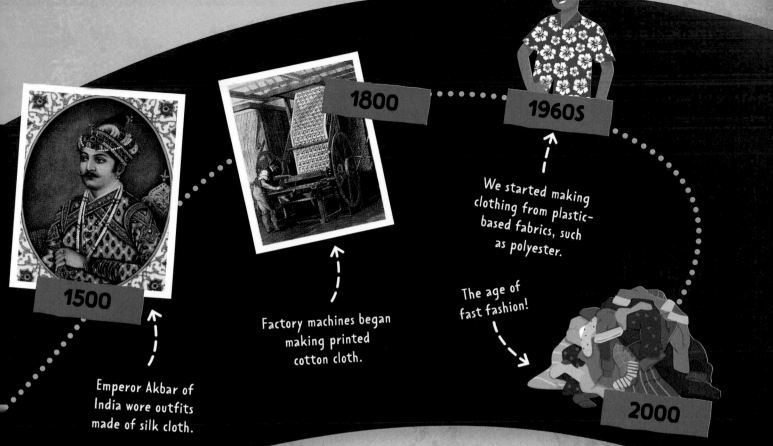

1500

1800

1960S

We started making clothing from plastic-based fabrics, such as polyester.

The age of fast fashion!

2000

Emperor Akbar of India wore outfits made of silk cloth.

Factory machines began making printed cotton cloth.

THROWAWAY FASHION

As clothes are cheap, people can buy more of them, even if they don't have much money. Clothes are often treated as disposable - sometimes, people wear them only once before throwing them away.

This means there's more demand - so more and more businesses and factories have been set up to make vast amounts of cheap, low-quality clothes.

This is known as 'fast fashion' - and of course, it's a sustainability disaster. It uses up raw materials and energy, and creates piles of waste.

SLOWING IT DOWN

Like other aspects of life, fashion can be made more sustainable if we switch to new ways of doing things.

★ Making better quality, longer-lasting clothes.

★ Recycling clothes and fabrics.

★ Reusing and reselling clothes, for example through charity shops or online selling sites.

★ Using natural fabrics instead of harmful plastics - especially sustainable fabrics made from weeds, leftover plant parts or plants that regrow almost as fast as they are used, such as bamboo.

GLOBAL WARMING

Global warming is one of the most dangerous changes our world has seen. The warming of the Earth is a result of pollution from human activities.

HOW DOES IT WORK?

The Earth is surrounded by an atmosphere – a layer of air, which is made up of a mixture of gases.

EARTH'S ATMOSPHERE

0.04% Carbon dioxide

21% Oxygen

78% Nitrogen

Less than 1% Other gases

GREENHOUSE EARTH

Some of the gases in the air, including carbon dioxide and methane, help to keep the Earth warm. They are called greenhouse gases, because the way they warm up the Earth works like a greenhouse.

This process, called the greenhouse effect, is natural and normal, and has always happened. It keeps the Earth warmer than it would be without an atmosphere.

1 Sunlight shines through

2 It heats up the ground and air

3 Some of the heat is trapped inside

GREENHOUSE GAS

However, since the Industrial Revolution started, we've been adding extra greenhouse gases to the air – mainly by burning fuel in our cars, factories, power stations and homes. When fuel burns, it releases carbon dioxide, an important greenhouse gas.

Another greenhouse gas, methane, comes from farm animals, especially cows. They burp it out as they digest their food. Other sources are rice farming and oil and gas drilling.

Pardon me!

CLIMATE EMERGENCY!

More greenhouse gases trap more heat, so the Earth's temperature has started to rise. This leads to a lot of problems ...

★ Hotter weather and dangerous heatwaves

★ More wildfires

★ More powerful hurricanes and storms, caused by heat making more seawater evaporate

★ Rising sea levels, as ice in glaciers and ice caps melts and runs into the sea.

We urgently need to cut down greenhouse gas release, before it's too late.

SUSTAINABLE ENERGY

One of the main reasons we burn so much fuel is to make electricity to power all our lights, machines and gadgets. To be more sustainable, we need to get electricity in other ways.

FUEL INTO ENERGY

Energy comes in several different forms, and can change from one form into another. Fossil fuels (oil, coal and gas) contain energy in the form of chemicals. A power station burns the fossil fuel and turns its chemical energy into a flow of electricity – another form of energy.

Pollution

Coal

Turbine

Pylons carry electricity

City

NO MORE FOSSIL FUELS

Burning fossil fuels is unsustainable in two main ways. Firstly, because it creates pollution and greenhouse gases. Secondly, because fossil fuels are going to run out! They are extracted from underground, where they formed millions of years ago. We don't have an endless supply.

RENEWABLE ENERGY

The sustainable solution is renewable energy. That means making electricity using energy sources, such as wind, sunshine and moving water, that don't get used up.

We're already using several types of renewable energy. To become sustainable, we need to switch to all renewable sources as soon as possible.

Another way to help the planet is to use less energy whenever we can. For example, by cycling or walking instead of going by car, and hanging washing out to dry instead of using a tumble dryer.

Actually, the Sun will run out of energy eventually – but not for at least another 5 billion years!

HYDROELECTRIC POWER

'Hydro' means water. A hydroelectric power station uses the downhill flow of water to make turbines spin and generate electricity.

SOLAR POWER

Solar panels turn energy from sunlight into a flow of electricity. A solar power station has vast sets of panels, but smaller panels can also be used on the roofs of houses and other buildings.

Wind turbines are like giant windmills. The wind makes them spin and machines called generators turn the spinning movement into electricity.

SEA POWER

We're already using wind, rivers and the Sun as renewable energy sources. But there's another vast source of sustainable energy waiting to be used: the sea.

The oceans' waves are a potentially huge source of energy.

SEA ENERGY

The sea's energy is found in the movement of its waves and tides. If you think about how much water the tides move up and down every day, and how big and powerful waves can be, that's a LOT of energy.

So far, though, we haven't used tidal or wave power as much as other types of renewable energy. Scientists and engineers have tried various ways to harvest the energy, but it's difficult to do. The sea is so powerful and unpredictable that energy-collecting devices often get damaged or stop working.

It's important to design sea power systems that don't harm local wildlife and habitats.

TIDAL POWER

One way to collect energy from the tides is to put turbines, which are similar to propellers, on the seabed. As the tide flows in and out, it pushes against the turbines, making them spin. Generators turn the spinning motion into electricity. However, turbines on the seabed can scare away or injure wildlife.

Another method is to let the tide fill up an artificial lake or lagoon, then let it flow out though turbines. Tidal lagoons are now being planned and built around the world.

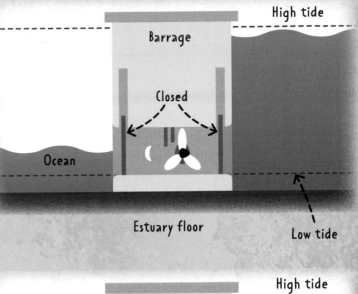

High tide

Barrage

Closed

Ocean

Estuary floor

Low tide

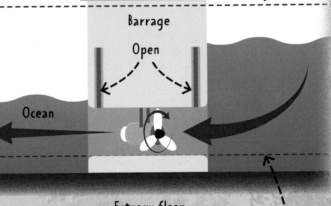

High tide

Barrage

Open

Ocean

Estuary floor

Low tide

Top is free to move up and down.

WAVE POWER

Screw

This part is anchored to the sea bed.

Wave power can work in various ways. One method uses special buoys with two parts. One part is anchored to the seabed. The other part floats, moving up and down as waves pass by. A screw-shaped part inside the fixed section turns the up-and-down movement into a spinning movement, which a generator turns into electricity.

TRANSPORT OF THE FUTURE

Cars, trains, ships and planes burn fuel, creating pollution and greenhouse gases. Yet we all rely on being able to travel from place to place. So, how can we make transport sustainable?

GO ELECTRIC

Electric vehicles reduce pollution as they run on a rechargeable battery instead of a fuel engine. However, to be sustainable, the electricity they use has to come from renewable sources (see pages 22-25).

We've already started switching to electric cars, buses and trains.

The first electric planes are on the way, too.

RECYCLE

We already reuse some metal and parts from old vehicles, but to be fully sustainable, we need to recycle all of it. The first 100% recyclable cars are being developed.

TRAVEL LESS

More people working from home

We zoom around to go to school, to work, on holiday and wherever else we like. We also transport food and other goods long distances around the world. Do we need to travel so much? We could reduce it by ...

Buying mainly local foods

Taking fewer, more local holidays

Making and transporting less stuff

FACT FILE

TRANSPORT TROUBLE

★ About 25% of greenhouse gases come from transport.

★ For each calorie of energy in the food we eat, up to ten calories are used to transport it.

★ The average American travels over 16,000 km by car each year.

HUMAN POWER

Walking, cycling and other types of human-powered transport don't cause any pollution or use any energy, except our own. We'll also be healthier if we move more!

HABITATS AND WILDLIFE

As the human population has grown, we have changed and damaged natural habitats all over the world, harming many of the species we share our planet with.

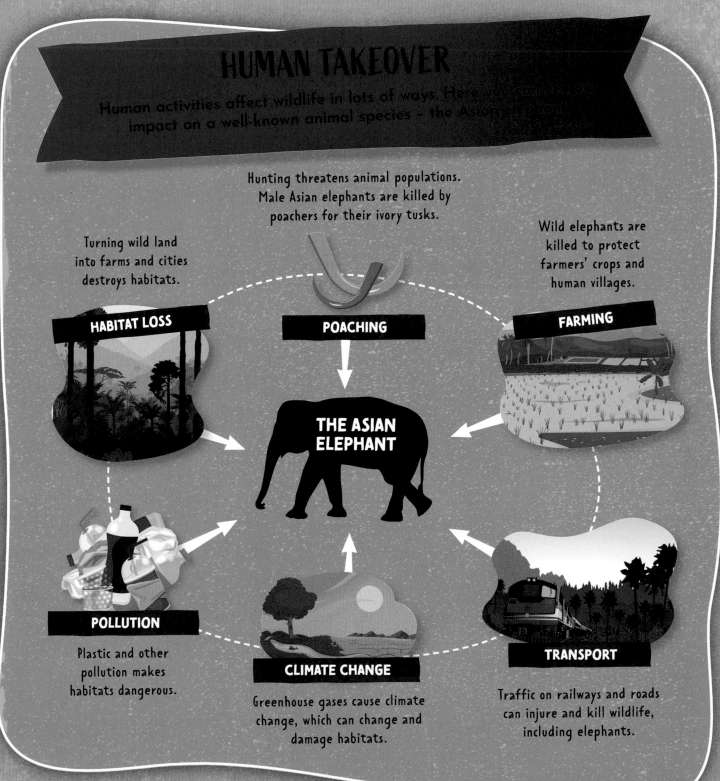

HUMAN TAKEOVER

Human activities affect wildlife in lots of ways. Here you can see their impact on a well-known animal species – the Asian elephant.

Hunting threatens animal populations. Male Asian elephants are killed by poachers for their ivory tusks.

Turning wild land into farms and cities destroys habitats.

Wild elephants are killed to protect farmers' crops and human villages.

HABITAT LOSS

POACHING

FARMING

THE ASIAN ELEPHANT

POLLUTION

Plastic and other pollution makes habitats dangerous.

CLIMATE CHANGE

Greenhouse gases cause climate change, which can change and damage habitats.

TRANSPORT

Traffic on railways and roads can injure and kill wildlife, including elephants.

ENDANGERED AND EXTINCT

Human activities have made some wild species extinct, while many more are endangered (at risk of dying out). Since 1964, the International Union for the Conservation of Nature (IUCN), has kept a 'Red List' of wild species that identifies endangered animals.

FACT FILE

ANIMALS IN DANGER

★ Over 32,000 species are listed as Vulnerable, Endangered or Critically Endangered, meaning they are threatened with extinction.

★ Creatures at risk include 26% of mammals, 41% of amphibians and around 33% of corals.

★ The Asian elephant has been listed as Endangered since 1986.

SOUTHERN CORROBOREE FROG
(Pseudophryne corroboree)

Status: CRITICALLY ENDANGERED
Location: AUSTRALIA
Class: AMPHIBIAN
Population: BELOW 100

WHAT CAN WE DO?

Almost everything we do affects the environment. We need to change our behaviour: cleaning up pollution, stopping climate change, using laws to protect animals and control hunting, and returning as much land as possible to a more natural state.

Nature reserves are protected areas where wildlife such as orangutans can live safely.

BIODIVERSITY AND ECOSYSTEMS

Biodiversity means the wide range of different species on Earth. It's important because the Earth and its living things work together as a system, called an ecosystem. Different things help each other to survive - for example, plants release oxygen that animals need to breathe, and animal droppings enrich the soil for plants. Losing species affects the balance and can harm other species (including us!).

FOOD AND FARMING

Around 12,000 years ago, people began farming. Now, as there are so many humans to feed, about 38% of the Earth's land surface has been turned into farms.

FARMS AND WILDLIFE

Farmland often has just one type of crop plant, such as bananas or wheat. This is called monoculture farming. Growing just one crop removes the variety of the natural ecosystem and natural pest-controlling insects.

A vast monocultural banana crop. - - -

FOOD PROBLEMS

Too much packaging

We often transport food long distances, using up energy and causing pollution. To be moved around, stored and sold in supermarkets, food has to be packaged, which creates waste.

Even worse, a lot of our food gets wasted – at least a third of it! It goes off and gets thrown away, or gets rejected for being the wrong shape or size.

A lot of food ends up rotting in landfill

'Wonky' vegetables are just as tasty

CARROTS

SUSTAINABLE FARMING

The good news is that we can make farming more sustainable, in several ways:

PLANT POWER

Farming animals uses up much more land and energy than growing crops. If people eat less meat and more plants, we can reduce the amount of farmland we need.

SUBSTITUTES

People are eating more plant-based meat substitutes and scientists are inventing ways to grow meat in labs, instead of raising and killing whole animals.

LOCAL FARMING

Eating food grown close to where you live saves energy and reduces pollution. In vertical farms, crops grow on shelves inside tall greenhouses, protected from pests. They don't need much land, so they can be located in or near cities.

EARTH-FRIENDLY FARMS

We can also farm in ways that help nature and ecosystems, for example:

★ Farming organically, without chemical pesticides and weedkillers

★ Collecting food and garden waste to make compost to enrich the soil naturally

★ Making space for wildlife on farmland, by keeping some wild areas, hedges and trees.

A hedgerow contains many different plant species, providing a habitat and food for birds, insects and small mammals.

31

AGROFORESTY

Imagine if a forest and a farm could be in the same place, so that we didn't need to cut forests down to create farms. Well, they can!

FOREST FARMS

Combining forests with farms is called agroforestry, from the word 'agriculture', meaning farming. You can combine trees and crops, or trees and animals.

For example, pigs are naturally forest animals. By keeping pigs in an orchard, you can use the same land for both pigs and a fruit crop. The trees also provide shade and a habitat for wildlife.

Pigs eat the leftover fruit, and their droppings can be used as fertiliser.

HILLSIDES OF HONDURAS

One famous type of agroforestry comes from Honduras in Central America. It's used in steep mountain areas where the climate is sometimes dry and sometimes stormy with heavy rain. It's called the Quesungual system after the village where it first began in the 1990s. Here's how it works:

1 Between the trees, farmers plant maize or bean crops.

3 Smaller trees are cut to a low height. The cut-off branches are used to cover the ground between the crop plants, which stops the soil from drying out.

2 Bigger trees produce fruit, nuts or seeds. They also protect the crops below from storms, and their roots stop soil from washing away.

AGROFORESTRY EVERYWHERE?

Agroforestry is a great way to make farming more sustainable in the future. It can be used around the world, as long as it combines types of trees, crops or animals that help each other and suit the local climate.

IT WORKS!

The Quesungual system is good for farmers and for the environment.

FARMERS GET:

★ Healthier soil

★ Better yield
(the amount of food they can grow)

★ Extra crops from the trees

★ A renewable supply of wood for building

★ A better income from selling their crops.

THE ENVIRONMENT GETS:

★ Habitats for wild species

★ Healthy soil for worms, fungi and bacteria

★ Trees that soak up carbon dioxide, reducing the greenhouse effect.

MAKING MONEY

In our world, almost everyone uses money. We do jobs to earn money and spend money to buy things. We can't really manage without it, but to be more sustainable we may need to make some changes.

BOOMING BUSINESSES

There are millions of businesses and companies in the world, large and small. They provide a service or product, such as painting houses, hosting websites or making fizzy drinks, and sell it to make money. Lots of people make a living from their own business, or by working for a business.

According to traditional economics – the science of money – businesses need to grow. A typical business tries to get more customers, make more money, and grow bigger and bigger. Businesses are seen as super-successful if they get really big and expand all over the world.

HANG ON A MINUTE!

The problem is that this is not very sustainable. Getting bigger and selling more means using up more resources, energy and space, and creating more pollution and waste. It may also mean putting other companies out of business, as you take their customers. This is why big businesses are always competing and taking each other over.

YEAR 1

YEAR 2

YEAR 3

YEAR 4

ROUND AND ROUND

In a sustainable world, business and money need to work differently. Instead of always trying to grow and make more and more profits, sustainable businesses need to be balanced and steady. Instead of using stuff up, they need to reuse old stuff so that it goes round and round, and use only renewable resources and energy. This is known as a circular economy.

As everything gets reused or is renewable, the system and the businesses in it can keep going without causing more and more problems for the Earth.

Instead of always trying to grow, companies can become more efficient, waste-free, green and sustainable.

THE CIRCULAR ECONOMY

MANUFACTURING

RECYCLING AND REUSE

SHORT-TERM TO LONG-TERM

In everyday life, we know the difference between the short term, or near future, and the long term, or more distant future.

SAVING UP

As an example, imagine you've got £50. You might be tempted to spend it all straight away on something fun and exciting.

But you'll probably realise it makes more sense to spend some now (the short term) and save some for later (the longer term). That way you can save up for other things and have some money left for emergencies.

SPEND IT ALL?

SAVE SOME?

RUNNING COUNTRIES

It's the same for governments who run countries. They need to think about the short-term and the long-term. However, most countries are democracies. This means people vote for their governments every few years.

Democracy means people can vote against a government and elect a new one. People can also choose between political parties with different ideas.

SHORT-TERM PROMISES

Unfortunately, this also means that many political parties make short-term promises to get elected. They try to appeal to voters in the present, instead of promising long-term changes.

VOTE FOR US!

We'll fund renewable energy research!

We'll make all cars electric!

We'll build more wildlife reserves!

LONG PARTY

VOTE FOR US!

We'll cut your taxes!

We'll create more jobs!

We'll build more houses!

SHORT PARTY

GOOD STUFF – NOW!

A LONGER VIEW

For the world to become sustainable, we need long-term planning too. That now is starting to happen. For example:

★ As people learn how important sustainability is, they are more likely to elect politicians with sustainability plans.

★ The United Nations (UN) holds regular sustainability conferences, where countries agree to commit to plans such as reducing greenhouse gases.

★ Protesters and campaigners persuade governments to switch to greener policies.

CLIMATE ACTION SUMMIT 2019

CLIMATE ACTION SUMMIT 2019

CLIMATE ACTION SUMMIT 2019

At the UN Climate Action Summit in 2019, 65 countries and regions agreed to reduce greenhouse gas emissions to zero by the year 2050.

HOW MANY PEOPLE?

Perhaps the biggest, most unsustainable problem of all is the number of humans on Earth. There are a lot of us!

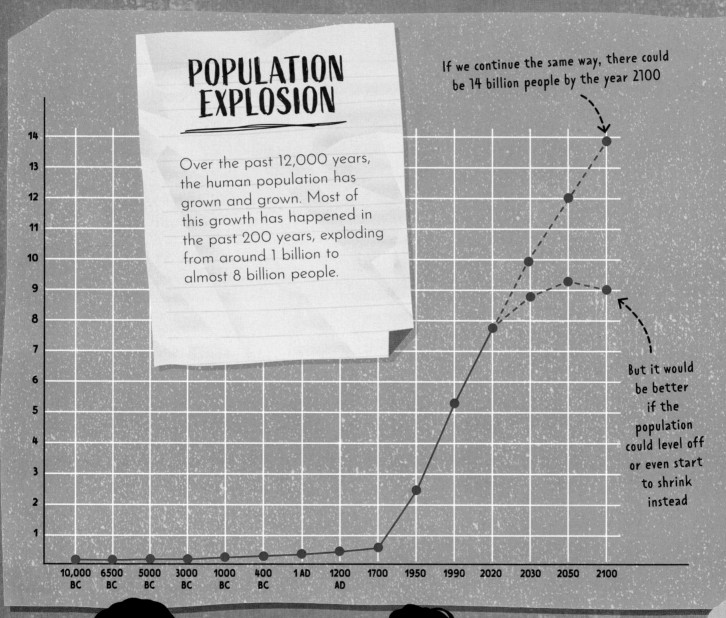

POPULATION EXPLOSION

Over the past 12,000 years, the human population has grown and grown. Most of this growth has happened in the past 200 years, exploding from around 1 billion to almost 8 billion people.

If we continue the same way, there could be 14 billion people by the year 2100

But it would be better if the population could level off or even start to shrink instead

SUSTAINABLE NUMBERS

If there were fewer people, it would be easier to live sustainably.

We'd need less food and water.

We'd take up less space with farms, cities and roads.

We'd use up fewer natural resources, such as plants and animals, minerals and fossil fuels.

We'd use less energy and release less pollution and greenhouse gases.

SHARING FAIRLY

Another problem is that some people and countries are wealthy, while others are poor. Sharing wealth more equally is an important part of sustainability. Reducing the population would make this easier, as there would be more resources to go around.

SHRINKING THE POPULATION

Population growth is already slowing in some places. This slow-down has been linked to better education and employment opportunities for women, and family planning schemes, meaning that women on average are having fewer children.

WHAT CAN YOU DO?

As you can tell from reading this book, we need to make a lot of changes to become truly sustainable. These changes involve almost every aspect of our lives. There's a LOT to do!

YOU CAN HELP!

These changes affect our everyday lives in many ways, so there are all kinds of ways you can help. Here are just some of them:

STUFF

★ Buy less new stuff if you can

★ Try to buy better-quality, longer-lasting products, and avoid disposable stuff

★ Look out for second-hand things, such as clothes and furniture

★ Recycle, reuse or pass on old stuff

★ Learn to mend things, so you don't have to throw them away

Try to mend clothes rather than always replacing them

GETTING AROUND

★ Get around by walking or cycling, if you can do so safely

★ Reduce long-distance trips

★ Travel by boat or train rather than by air

★ Have some holidays closer to home

★ If you need a family car, could you switch to an electric one?

Try exploring your own country or area.

Eat more vegetables.

FOOD

★ Eat less meat, or even go vegetarian

★ Choose locally grown and seasonal food if you can

★ Avoid over-packaged food, or choose recyclable packaging

★ Reuse shopping bags or boxes.

Reusable shopping bags save on waste plastic.

AT HOME

★ Save energy by turning off lights and appliances when you're not using them

★ If possible, switch from gas to electricity for heating and cooking

★ Recycle whatever you can: paper, card, glass, cans, plastic and food waste

★ If you have a garden, let some of it grow wild to help wildlife.

★ Plant a tree if possible!

Plant a tree and watch it grow!

THE FUTURE...

As you get older, you'll make decisions about your life. Will you have children? How many? What job will you do? Where will you live? Though you might not always be able to make the most sustainable choice, you can think about sustainability whenever you're faced with a decision.

A SUSTAINABLE FUTURE

What will our future look like? If we make everything as sustainable as we can, it could look something like this.

IN THE CITY

Cities could be smaller, with vertical farms and agroforests in and around them to provide food.

ENDLESS ENERGY

All our energy would come from renewable sources: wind farms, solar and hydroelectric power stations, wave and tide power – and maybe new methods still to be invented.

NOTHING WASTED

All the materials we use would be recycled and reused in a circular economy. Food and plant waste would be turned into compost to improve the soil.

WILDER WORLD

Existing pollution would be cleaned up, and polluting products such as plastic bags would no longer be made. We would eat less meat, so there would be less animal farming, fishing and hunting.

The seas would be cleaner and less polluted. There wouldn't be any oil spills, as oil would no longer be needed.

SEAS AND OCEANS

A FAIRER WORLD

With fewer people, and mainly plant-based farming, there would be more space, food, clean water and materials to share out equally.

WILL IT HAPPEN?

We're already taking the first steps towards a world like this, but we have to hurry up! The changes need to happen as soon as possible, so that we can live on a safe, clean planet – for us, for other living things, and for the humans of the future.

GLOSSARY

Agroforestry Combining forests with farmland for growing crops or keeping animals.

Antibiotics Medicines that kill bacteria, used to treat many illnesses.

Atmosphere The layer of air around the Earth.

Biodiversity The variety of living things in a particular habitat, or in the whole world.

Calorie A unit of energy, used to measure the energy in food or fuel, or the energy used up by activities.

Carbon dioxide (CO_2) A gas found in the air, and released when carbon-based fuels burn.

Circular economy A system of making and selling things that recycles the same materials and avoids waste and pollution.

Climate change A long-term change in Earth's climate and weather patterns.

Compost Rotted plants or leftover food, used for improving soil.

Consumer Someone who buys or uses things.

Democracy A country or state where people vote to elect the government.

Disposable Made to be thrown away after use.

Economic To do with money and wealth, and how they move around in society.

Economics The study or management of the way money and wealth work.

Economy The system of money, wealth, buying and selling in a country, or in the whole world.

Ecosystem A particular habitat, area or place and all the living things that are found there.

Endangered At risk of dying out and becoming extinct.

Energy The power to make things happen or do work.

Environment The surroundings, especially natural surroundings or the natural world.

Environmental movement A political movement, originating in the 1800s, that aims to protect the natural environment, or surroundings.

Extinct An extinct species is one that has died out and no longer exists.

Fossil fuels Fuels such as coal, oil and gas, formed underground from animals or plants that died long ago.

Generator A device that turns a spinning motion into a flow of electricity.

Global warming A gradual increase in Earth's average temperature over the last two centuries, caused by human activities.

Green A word used to mean aware of the need to reduce damage to the planet.

Greenhouse effect The way some gases in the Earth's atmosphere trap heat, increasing global warming.

Greenhouse gases Gases that contribute to the greenhouse effect, such as carbon dioxide and methane.

Green movement Another name for the environmental movement.

Habitat The natural home or surroundings of a living thing.

Hedgerow A thick line or row of different types of trees and bushes, used to separate fields or other areas.

Holocene epoch The name for the period of time since humans began farming, about 12,000 years ago.

Hydroelectric power Electricity produced from the movement of flowing water.

Industrial Revolution A period of major development around the world, starting in the 1700s, towards using factories, machines, engines and electricity in manufacturing and transport.

Internal combustion engine A type of engine that burns fuel to power cars and other vehicles.

Landfill A site, or hole in the ground, where rubbish is piled up, then covered over.

Methane A greenhouse gas often used as a fuel, and also produced by farm animals such as cows.

Monoculture Farming a single crop or type of animal over a large area.

Nature reserve A natural wild area that is set aside and protected to stop it from being changed or damaged by humans.

Oxygen A gas found in the air, which animals breathe in to make their cells work.

Population Number of people.

Raw materials Basic, unchanged materials that are used to make things.

Renewable energy Energy sources that do not run out, such as wind, waves and sunshine.

Resources Stocks or supplies of something, such as water, fish, or wood from trees.

Social To do with society, or groups of people and how they behave.

Solar panel A panel of material that converts sunlight into an electric current.

Species The scientific word for a particular type of living thing.

Sustainable Able to be continued in the same way over a long time.

Sustainable development Improving and developing the way we live in a sustainable way.

Synthetic Artificial, or made by humans, by processing and changing raw materials.

Taxes Money that people and businesses pay to their government to help run their country.

Tidal lagoon A human-made enclosure that catches sea water when the tide comes in, then uses it to turn turbines to produce electricity.

Turbine A device that uses a movement, such as the flow of wind or water to make a wheel spin, which is then used to generate electricity.

Vertical farm An indoor farm where crop plants are grown in trays on several levels.

Wilderness A wild, natural area that has not been damaged or taken over by people.

Wildlife reserve A kind of nature reserve set aside to provide a safe home for wildlife.

Wind turbine A turbine powered by the wind.

Yield The amount of food or other products that come from a farm.

FURTHER READING

BOOKS

OUR PLANET:
The one place we all call home

By Matt Whyman and Richard Jones (Harper Collins, 2019)

Stunning photos, maps and beautiful illustrations celebrating the world of nature.

PROTECT THE PLANET:
How to be kind to our world and change the future

By Jess French (Dorling Kindersley, 2021)

How young people today can change the world to create a greener, sustainable future.

101 SMALL WAYS TO CHANGE THE WORLD

By Aubre Andrus (Lonely Planet Kids, 2018)

Lots of fun, simple, practical ideas for making everyday changes to make the world more sustainable.

GUARDIANS OF THE PLANET:
How to be an Eco-Hero

By Clive Gifford and Jonathan Woodward (Buster Books, 2019)

A positive look at how children can become protectors of the planet.

WEBSITES

kids.nationalgeographic.com/nature/save-the-earth

National Geographic Kids Save the Earth website, with activities, quizzes and lots of information.

climatekids.nasa.gov/

Climate Kids, a NASA website about climate change, how it works and how we can fight it.

www.kidsagainstplastic.co.uk/

Campaign to reduce plastic use and plastic pollution, with activities, facts and ideas.

WATCH

Our Planet (2019) by Silverback Films, narrated by David Attenborough

TV series exploring the natural world and the impact of human activities, including climate change.

Watch it on Netflix, and online at https://www.netflix.com/gb/title/80049832

Tomorrow (Demain) (2019) by Cyril Dion and Mélanie Laurent.

French documentary about some of the many changes people are making around the world to create a more sustainable future.

Watch it on Amazon Prime Video or Apple TV

INDEX